MINed MUzzle velociTy

MINed MUZZle veLociTY

JENNIFER H. FORTIN

Lowbrow
Press

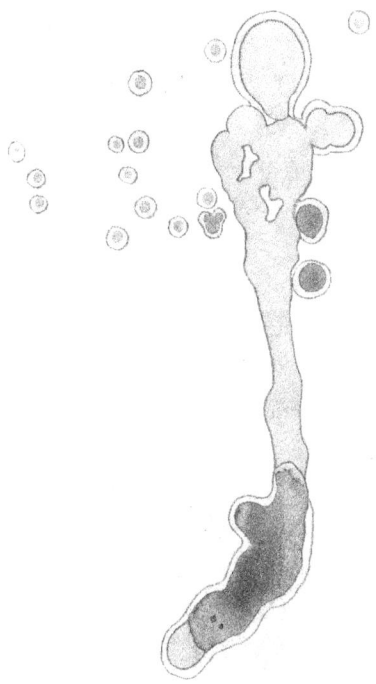

Cover design: Jana Vuković

Published by Lowbrow Press
www.lowbrowpress.com

ISBN 978-0-9829553-5-2

For my mother & my father

Mined muzzle velocity

Dear,   October

Late last night a stranger told me (we were
both influenced) he Liked my shoes & Get
home safe. Mostly when the lights
are on nobody is home, I said. Thought that
was a good response, but he looked
surprised. I hope one day to be read
my rights. I will talk along & it will almost
be like I have a voice. Food here is deathly,
even arriving with no expectations. This is
not one of those terrible free postcards.
Really—look at the front. It's clumsy that
you have to stop the mail when someone
dies. Imagine that conversation.

Surely things keep coming years after.
There are land mines; their violence is
indiscriminate, whereas knives & guns

_____
_____
_____

require real time. I hope not to detonate.
This is a hopeful postcard!
Running out of room—pls. watch
the mail—I have something I want to show
(you may recall how I don't believe in
envelopes).
Yrs. (I always write in the part they cover
up.)

Dear,   October

Dry little blades will mow down a stray
naked foot, fitting reversal not to be
We had a tree until poor   blamed.
structure killed. Each neighborhood
shadeless lawn crisped, mourned what had   _____
creaked overhead.   _____
Now the flattened plots without root, some _____
outdoor vestibule
missing the relief of above   Poor structure affects any home's
slight pressure   circumference.
emanating the base. Neat stump—   Bury this in your gut. Take preventative
aggression's residue. Outdoor ceilingless   measurements
vestige, futile,   & venerate your vegetable radius.
trying to welcome, to say *Come in.*
                                         Say hi to everyone. Yrs.

                                         P.S. Do you know your blood group?
                                         Transfusion can be fatal. Do you know
                                         my blood group?

Dear,   November

Been meaning to tell you—Emily D. likes
a look of agony. I do, too. Offers much
opportunity for empathy. Agony
so close to apology. One time I'd like you
to apologize & not stick around
for acknowledgment. That's okay.
Sometimes it is not fine. Jimmy up
the block (I think?) told me I was pretty,
waited for thanks & modified
with ugly. Pretty ugly. Marched over
with Mom & she made him say Sorry, &
when I said That's okay, No it's not,
she said. Twice wrong. Anyway, you
were wondering: Dear, you never were
dearest.

I had a dream & kept calling you

Appliance Face. That look of agony
on any device put into contact
with something. Countertops
teeming with microscopic filth. Am I
making any sense? I want our relations
peaceful. Amity as between nations,

_____
_____
_____

documented & official, having passed
through designated stages, ratified. I
don't even know how all that works.
Are you at home much these days?
If you leave for long stretches, you can
stop your mail. You just have to give
them dates. So no one sees the dangerous
pileup & has no-good thoughts.
The Jimmy thing was years ago.
Yrs.

Dear,   November

Greetings. Weather is iffy & ill-timed.
& there? When was the last time you felt
amorous enough to do something about it?
Curious. Have you ever been
decorated? Maybe medals & honors
delineate the amorphous. Maybe. I
struggle with so many things. Seems you
do, too. There's the agony for you. Right
now I share a window with a stranger, not
a wall. I'm probably more apt to run into a
wall than a window. I bet the plaster ones
wish they were anatomical: abdominal
wall. Or metaphorical. Wall of silence.
Sorry, didn't notice your wall of silence.

I can't really remember what I am trying
to. Well, I've been pondering
the desire to take the window seat.
The prized window seat. The only thing
I can come up with is it helps to be
separate from the outside while inside with
a thickness of slow-moving

_____

_____

_____

glass. In a way, the window is a wall, too.
You prefer that position over
the deeper-in. It gets unnatural, you say.
Let's meet up for dinner if I ever come
back. There's a prime repertoire of sensual
events. It's just unclear as to whether
agony is included or not. Alright, I'm off.
Yrs.
What's your perspective on clarity?

Dear,   November

What do you think of the statue?
Nothing like it in the world. I walked
all the way around & touched
when the guard had turned back. Fawn
Seeking Favor. Oh, Dear, I could not help
but think of you. The guard concealed
his weapon & I risked a great deal.
Have I shown you the real skeleton key
I have? It is filed but opens no real locks.
It is real, though. Are you asking
where the name came from. Well,
my guess is it is supposed to support
what is softest, like any closet.
Are you asking if I tried between
the fawn's pursed, fur-locked lips because
it begged in behavior. I could have risked
a great deal. You named it. All faucets
I try lately—dried up. Do not
remember what it is to have moist breaks.
& the size of my body is the size of my

bed. Nothing is easy, yous. This IS
meant for yous. I was saying, though:
the intensity fawn. Look for it
online, maybe. Are you asking if I get
all your e-mails. Do you send them?
Last time I checked, I had thousands
in bulk. One from Conscious—Shed It,
I was encouraged. Like a grown male

_____

_____

_____

heady growth. Do not look for it online—
nevermind. You need to see these things
in the round. Plans for Thanksgiving?
Are you really asking thanks
this year. I do not know where I sleep.
As always, I remain Yrs.
Enveloping prevents openness to sky.
I suggest you quell all urges
to encase but not to enumerate.
As in: count on, but do not close on.

Dear,   November

Yo. What do you do with your time
there? Even rituals, evening rituals.
People here are harsh in theory
& practice, continuous-tense.
Wherever I go looking for goods,
I am forced to ask them to check
the back, as the shelves are empty.
& there is always more behind.
You said once if you check the mailbox
& do not like the prospect, you close
the top & leave it. Close the top & leave
it. The papers present platitudes as news.
Announcement of threat can be none,
as with the diminutive poisonous.
Have you been working on your
invective? Not to be rude, but because
I care for it. As opposed to *don't*

care for. Speaking of don't care for,
I do not know whether I mean I do not
like (blank) or I do not have feelings
for (blank). Example: no, thank you, I *do
not care for* threatening,
non-obvious situations. At times,

_____
_____
_____

the oddest apocryphal wind blows
indoors & causes shut ups. I assume
all is well with you. April is coming up;
be thinking about taxes, write-offs &
demands. I sure am.
& hey, how about making anything
a little less harrowing for me?
No? Well, what can I do?
Yrs.

Dear,   November

This made me think of you.
Don't know how much longer I'll be here/
how much more I can take. A person told
me I had eaten plenty holiday & I breathed,
how much? The amount *one* can want
fails to account for me. Know what I mean?
I can't help many things about myself.
Look at the moat. We fit ourselves
btwn. concentric moats, target-like. Gives
us aim & opportunity to test. The bulls-
eye, both least & most vulnerable at once.
Cross the ditches, get anywhere unless you
need to circle, to keep moving. I find I can't
help but erase the history on my cell
phone. Try never to call me. Went on
a spree & painted the sensitive town red
after possibly overdoing it on exceeding-

ly tasty meat. The fattest proportion
of stories = one's own self interspersed w/
a mad enhanced bull. I wish I knew
your agenda these days & whether you
wear costume when violating givens. Today
is Everything-Appreciation Day,
or so it seems. The rotten leftover.

_____

_____

_____

How are rehearsals? Working toward
demolition after the applause? I stopped
that years ago, or so I like to think.
Nearly forgot—when I needed to gain
entrance to the Fawn, I had misplaced my
ticket & the doorman (literally) looked
the other way as I slipped by. It works.
Enthusiastically, Yrs.
Remarkable undereye circles now

Dear,   November

This one—more critical. After almost
deciding to call it a day, I felt I needed
to write: remember when your selflessness
was displayed in notable contrast to my
selfishness? Remember when you knew
the situation through me, only through me,
& so it had glaring effect, your offer
to accompany me there. Remember I said no
it takes forever to get to that place.
That was appalling.
Remember I went to the bathroom directly.
To brush my teeth, gain a taste
& I don't know if you could hear me,
but I went too far & gagged, basically
losing it into the plugged-up sink,
slow & old. Exiting, you never
would have guessed from my face,
or the glint of my breath, because

I did not, in fact, end up yakking.
Remember or did this not occur. Did
the dreams not start again which wake me
at inconvenient hours. In neck-sweat
& freaked the fuck out, but that's more about
me (again) than the ones it's really about.
Little vials you take in a certain order,

_____
_____
_____

friendly promises of The Other Side.
Well, just remembering.
The ins & outs of effect. Studies
in contrast & gesture.

Pls. don't spread it around, impatience &
neglect, Yrs.

Dear,   January

Dying to get back ~~the~~ in touch.

Happy with the news?

_____
_____
_____

                              Yrs.

9

Dear,   January

I write from the divide. My axis is still
crooked—yours? Giving
the humid hips again?

I thought you knew that people do not own
axes & my heat is concentrated imaginary.
Remember how cold it was to cast
no shadow?

Enough of that. Been to many
interviews lately. Not sure for what title,
but the subordinate always manages
to make itself evident, someone

commanding someone. Human Resources
the most hidden & shapely department.

I think of the postcard as a sideways
call to action. Untangle nets & shine
your minute fort. It starts to smart
after you see blood. It continues

_____
_____
_____

smarting when I see anything's blood.

Do you suppose this is working out?

Racked with Uncertainty & Affect, Yrs.

Dear,   January

Familiar or unfamiliar with the payment
procedure? The currency here will remain
at body temperature if you
tuck it in your sock. Methinks that is how
the culture validates.

& what about that visit? I'll show you
everything or as much as I can.

_____

_____

_____

Flowing in a Medium Kind of Way, Yrs.

Dear,   January

Sorry not to have addressed you
more recently: Do you know details
of the first animal sacrifice? Dear,
the goat gnawed a farmer's grape leaves
& he killed the goat in rage. Horrified,
the farmer concluded that a ritual
would balance his act, completing
with eating. Still like your meat
well done? Is there not nowhere else
to go these days but extremes? Do you
find your outrage/hatred justified?
When driving your car, as the driver,
there is a best way to hit a sudden deer.
Let up on the brakes

so the headlights tilt slightly upward into
their normal stance. Has this move ever
saved your life? Would you want it to?
Maybe would that be a good way to go.

_____
_____
_____

We need context to plait.
Brakes lower the headlights if pressed.
True or not: to occur is to note
a pre-existing situation. Were you ever
into assembly? What if you join together
multiple stiff fibers? I'm not certain
roads are always a good way out.
Nebulously, Yrs.

Dear,   January

Welcome, yous! We extend our
acceptance. We extend our
acknowledgment. We extend our
advice, dismissal & encouragement.
We extend our deepest love, regret,
goodwill & several job offers. We
extend a somber farewell. We extend
embarrassed termination. We extend
an unlikely business deal. We excel
in sales. We extend convincing
recommendation. We extend a get-well,
probably called for after our ruthless
past reprimands. We extend sincere
inquiry as to your previous errors &
ours. We extend our extensions. We are
getting thin. We introduce ourselves.
We have reservations for & about
social events. We extend them. We

_____

_____

_____

have been planning this for so long.
How unfathomable that it could actually
happen now.

Keen & Easy Condolences, Yrs.

Dear,   January

This one was expensive, Dear, I hope
you hang it up. Which side?
Problems that seem like design flaws
are actually your own problems most
of the time. The people here are into
concepts. Concept albums, concept cars,
concept homes. They want to gauge
reaction & hold safety panels. They
like to draw up contracts based on chance.
I can't quite sign. How is your recall
doing? The people here recall tiny
particulars. Is that important to you?
Did I persuade you with my last missive
or did you cycle around it? Or did you

collapse with worry after reading it?
Do not fret, do not fret, Dear. Yrs. retains
glinty fervent gleam o'
the eye. I'm certain you retain that casual
attitude toward takeoff & landing.
My exit doors may or may not work

_____

_____

_____

in the unlikely event of an emergency.
How's that for a concept.

For your information:
the dreams have not ceased.

I am beat. Yrs.
P.S. Are you intrigued by an adventurous
body? Should you be?

Dear,   January

We have the same infirmities
as most others. What do you say
we get together sometime & avoid
talking about it?

_____

_____

_____

Less Than Wan, Yrs.

15

Dear, January Hey. How *are* you? I was so lucky today to witness grazing wild. Imagine us bending like that: Descent into the Rations, I'd call it. Hosting institutions coordinating sneaky shifts for precisely those moments. To feed is exposure. Abnormal when we do it in company. White fur throat to catch things not white. Perhaps a skittish white heart trotting within—how could we find out? You seem widely distributed.	The hyperhidrosis: should I take it as aggression? Or is it one of the sources of your quotidian humiliations? Getting so mixed up. _____ _____ _____ You now seem somewhere between. Time to rub my nose in dinner of a certain height. Yrs.

Dear,   January

        THE LARGER THE ANIMAL
        THE LARGER THE RUB

                                          _____
                                          _____
                                          _____

                                Obviously Yrs.

Dear,   January

If you're like me, you have less time
than ever. The vehicles here are
interesting, & the signs. Billboards
shout business, Frozen Chickens,
Fresh Eggs (?). Vans transporting, &
recklessly. Lane markers are futile.
The vehicles decked out
with mottos. Best one:

Let Them Say

The airplane flew here in order to be
fixed.

A question for you: is restless leg
syndrome worse when you have more
than 2 legs? Spindly small grace,
cannot stop the motions. Anatomy
vital for placement education.

_____

_____

_____

Today the tailor came to measure me
for traditional attire. This will be a great
honor, but more than anything, I want
an intact arrival. You never said:
ARE you like me?
Crashing, Yrs

Dear, January	
I am realizing I may be in your territory. I may be a visitor. I will detect the wind's direction & take odors into account.	_____ _____ _____
	In a Kind of Rut, Hungry, Confused, Yrs.

Dear, January	
Needless to say	——————————— ——————————— ———————————
	Under Optimal Conditions?, Yrs.

Dear,   January

Don't you like to learn new facts, mined
& specific? Explode out reports.
I think I do. Relating, being held
accountable. Learn about the hunters
in order to exact revenge.

Dear, do you overpopulate? Organize
about it. May I suggest you draft
a new constitution & peer ever vigilant.
All affairs are to be taken seriously.

People tend to remember last times if
prodded. If too long goes by, will you
forget the last time? The last time we
saw each other. Or they embed,
burrowing parasites, live dependently
& harm. Declare your independence?
Let's each report on the enemy crouch.
Brainstorm, use trees & clouds to think.

_____
_____
_____

I knew you'd appreciate the flipside
of this. Subsets can be beautiful
& surprise. Basically, Yrs.

Dear,   January

Seen any movies out now? Do ticket-
checkers even let you in? I'm sure you
could make a case for looking different
& filling many grace seats. You would
not understand the adult content &
strong language, unless there were
predators involved. (Almost wrote:
"inloved." What do you make of
underground inclinations? Weird,
intimate writhing down there.)

_____
_____
_____

I thought I'd have more to say. I shall
recline, climb, bring on the clinical.
Is it acceptance or exceptance? You
would know in a heartbeat. I would
too. Increasingly faulty faculties, Yrs.

Dear,   January | Radiating roads position one well
                                        | for military action. It is cold here,
As someone aware of inspiration | & I don't have filters left in my drawer.
of the limp, I know you face some | I feel April's deft slide under my anxious.
extremely difficult situations. Impairment
can alter how we increase. Impairment | _____
can branch off into span. Impairment can| _____
eat the optimal. Impairment can point you| _____
out as the primary culprit, can ask: who is| Asked you to consider taxes. Did you?
the sufferer? Impairment is survey. | The seasons will turn, as thought & back.
Impairment still likes crops & bounding | We charge only those aware of violation.
into roads. Impairment's density is like| As we already confirmed: you are aware
the non-trees between other trees. Fence,| of a type of inspiration. Will you
trap, repel, transfer. Experiments in | recognize your life's loudest noise
monitor & less hoofing it. | when you hear it? Superlatively, Yrs.

Dear,   January

I've travelled to a new emotional lodge,
I write you from it. You skewer me, you
suspend me & I am not clear; that's okay
for now? How are your emotions—
cosmopolitan? Metabolizing, bucking?
Maintain, velvety edge.

Talked with another traveller yesterday:
she said she Almost forgot about
the theory of evolution. Moving, as much
as any animal power.

Problematic—we tend to equate
intellectual abilities with the ability
to read & write. Dilemma tales, trickster

tales to tell. Attended a weaving workshop.
Looms clacked while bush fires nearby
cracked. Workers there got paid not by
hours worked, but by cloth produced.
You work 4 contraptions with bare feet
& weave with your hands. You can't do it.

_____
_____
_____

Tonight I will take any host family out
for a thank you dinner. We will go to
Chances. Busy, tired, learning, engulfed.
Tomorrow I may depart again, board
some bumpy bus.

Soon: Yrs.

Dear,   January

When in another place, you just get
proposed to more often. Do you find this
to hold true when you crowd new land?
How does the native sweat skin onto you?
I am now at a resort, which allows
for delicious sluggishness. Resort to
the eyes on the sides of your head. Resort
to camouflage incisor. Resort to
a responsive palate & what it is you
consume. Tentative to name specifics, but
I spotted a crocodile in the water. Then
had a urinate adventure behind a wall with
Nikki & Maya, not so heroic here. I am
with others, & also I am not with others. I
have no idea how I feel about you.
Facilities, unreliable.

Dilemma of a Ghost, a play in 3 acts.
You like plays. Here, performances are
communal activities; no defined audience,
but participatory. Are you indifferent to
participation? Got a hunch you are.
Have you ever tried to develop sth. that is

_____

_____

_____

your own through a language not your
own? It stabs without wounding. Yes,
let us name names & sort once more, let us
appeal frequently to relaxation, a business
proposal for the dissection.

Hunching along timorously, Yrs.

Dear,   January

Hi, there, formulaically.

Authenticity claims the peculiar should fit
the group. Themes can be universal, a
single turn. Happy Birthday vernacularly
translates to You must be lucky to be alive
today. Audiences & hunters do not come
to the performance with blank minds.
The live feats—ephemeral. Shorthand
of actual meaning. Change the act
from time to time: account for change
& transition. Freezes, otherwise. Get with
the holistic program. No individual claims
copyright or ownership because
the community supports him. Meaningful
only in a communal

setting. Did you bring the tissues & your
lucky feet, different. You bear unique
responsibility. Come to my concert party, it
promises the religious & the secular. We
could use discussion catalysts. Attack root
causes, not symptoms. The play is not
finished until the problem has ended.

_____
_____
_____

I think you would appreciate it, as a lover
of shedding & information. I write this from
my numbered seat, doing an excellent job,
as usual, of getting in the way.

Wish you were here, kind of, Yrs.

Dear, January	personal relationships noise handling noise the missionary noise the super-evident
In closing, I greet you. Traditional music is so important because it provides idiom. Non-musical groups like hunters & warriors needed their own music related to events. In contemporary society, no event is necessary. I'm all for re-contextualization.	noise noise of backs noise of obligation noise of ethnicity noise of school noise of someone noise of good
	_____
	_____
	_____
I'm all for cross-rhythms, how your tiny feet amplify polyrhythmic. Everyone is expected to take part, but to varying degrees. Let's all get chief knowledge & beat it out.	song of quotation song of pages song of digits song of the wandering song of method song of residential areas' safety song of exclusion song of young hidden song of breeding rights song of the raised song of availability song of the downest fur song of the atonal song of Yrs. song
insult noise lover noise politics noise inter-	

Dear,   January

Learn the song yet? Or do you not sing?
Apprenticeship yet, in any sector at all?
We are forced to use intermediaries to
communicate due to our imperfect state.
Would you risk disaster by working on
a sacred day? Would others believe you
risked disaster? Occupied with these
things. Are there curses in the woods?
Chambered corners? Are you conscious
of your ancestors? Do you worship them?
Do they punish you? What about our
ancestors? Do they punish you?

I saved you a program. Here:
1. Arrival of Visitors.

2. Exchange of Greetings.
3. Pouring of Libation.
4. Musical Interlude.
5. Introductions.
6. A Talk.
7. Adorning of Visitors.
    _____
    _____
    _____
8. Musical Interlude.
9. WELCOME on Multiple Behalves.
10. Refreshment/Musical Interlude.
11. Distribution of Visitors.
12. Vote of Thanks.
13. Departure.

You Have My #12, for Being There, Yrs.

Dear,   January

When you entered your office & absorbed
your assistant's ashen face, you instantly
discerned the dynamic of letting go.
It happened when the shrines turned
into tourist attractions.

This day has been so long. They always are
when you are travelling within travels.
Maybe you don't even notice. The pursuit
moon slams at our sensations. The sand is
dry like it should be, comfortable, with
useful shells. Have you run on the sand
before? I know you enjoy swimming &
quickly. You, brutalized by others
who name you Stubborn. They name you
Pest & Ruinous to planned ornamental

patterns. They name you Gasp & Bullet.
You are discussed, conferenced. Some
evidence lives. Let's check in as a group.

_____
_____
_____

(in transit)

At least knock on a tree, send me
some signal, Yrs.

29

Dear, January	
Dear, Dear, me. I left again. Have you?	_____ _____ _____ It's Started Already, Yrs.

Dear,   January

Placid hellos, yous. How are you?
I purchased a gift for the next ones:
wind chimes, celestial, & a jar of peanut
butter. I'll be revealed as either strange
fool or faintly astute. I'm sure a bit of both
at various points of this leg. I left packing
for the night before. I feel very prepared,
but not over-prepared. Goodbyes were
nothing to write home about, except that
resilient happy spilled gesture from some.
The driver came to a stop at a light on
the way to the airport, & there's Tony at
the corner gas station, pumping gas.
Underscore of our unlike situations.

Now, stuck in inexplicable state of
neutrality. You are the one scraping
the ground. Mathematical seclusions
explain why we go curvy. At orientation, I
will scope out possibility. Feeling a bit
more part of the mechanism. Lanterns,
squares.

_____

_____

_____

Today was monument roof: open to
the public only once/year. By the way,
cash machines aren't compatible here with
cards. How do you defend screenless
windows? With voluminous vim, Yrs.

Dear,   January

Where to begin? There was a general
meeting of two with a moment of silence.
Or a silence of two with a moment of
general meeting. It was horrible. Where
were you when it happened? Maybe it only
happened to me. Yes. You don't even
know, Dear, because I haven't told anyone
what happened. Where were you when it
happened? Spooked, I ran for miles &
kilometers & could have used you. Next
time we take part of him, his upper lip &
stiff, as vile trophy. Tonight I anticipate
a focused air of study in this room: not
necessarily denial or forgetting, but
a rigorous challenging of energy. Tonight I

remain under excavated fury:
the intruder's labor did not end
when he thought it did.

Tonight I memorize utilitarian phrases
of deflection & defense.

_____
_____
_____

Enough repetition of his stupid jean jacket,
Yrs.

Dear,   January

If you've been worried about the herd
sweeping you up into nothing, I've got
advice for you. Keep your gaze
focused on a single object below
the horizon, like a vault or transept, even
if invisible. Travel from town to town
in this manner, trust me. Maybe you can't.

Meant to tell you in the last one: things
occur in broadest daylight, too. I know your
affection toward dusk, night & dawn, but
they strike at all times. Be careful. Stay
angry. Do not pause if you don't catch
the question the first time around.

I strongly recommend a tour of
the amphitheatre previously used for blood
sports. You tenderly beg for the iron
deposits found, to this day, in the clay. I
thought of you the entire time there,
eating handfuls of dirt.

_____
_____
_____

How long after not seeing, hearing, or
smelling danger is it advised to wait until
returning to a routine?

Our strengths are different?,
Our weaknesses are different?,
Our legs are different, Yrs.

Dear,   February

Well, well. Firsts can scream something,
although weird we default back to them.
Reset. Weather here today. There?
Does it thirst you to lick tingle minerals?
Make you thirst for more. Salubrious
saline of nutrient. We mimicked & thrust
into plastic hospital bags, operative.
Attractive blocks for the sculpting, you
nature artist, along the game trail. My
guilt-jacket's houndstooth sports jagged
hunt teeth. I alternate between it, my
careful cloak, others & nudity. Rate each
saliva drop, my Dear, & what its attire.

I may be in deface mode these days, &
it scares even me. February feels peculiar,
the valves.

Will take a turn somewhere now.

_____
_____
_____

The Resistance, Yrs.

Dear,   February

Researched your social behavior & mis-,
also ventured on expedition here
(distraction). Went after music drift
sidestreet to a crowd. Middle-aged man
w/ black floppy shoes, black worn suit,
tape playing on a deck. Police drove
through & tried to break up the show—
impossible. Then the mustache pulled me
up there. Had me stand still, hands at
sides, look up. Pulled a handkerchief &
more from under my top. Then returning
witnessed accident: a moped run into,
driver sit up & then crumple again. To tell
an officer, we interrupted a conversation
he held with a black-eye man. We ditched
& happened (more later)

Upon various stone walls graffitied
fascism concerns. Are you alert to antis &
pros? Then I went alone to a jazz club—2
guitar men. How would you take that?
Muddy? Sometime this week I'd like to
examine the famous crypts. I will pry it
out of the faces there, returning
to the above past: inept badge forces,

———————————————
———————————————
———————————————

the return accident, jazzy black-eye
fascist teeming. Coax anything from
under my top, the criminal & cop.
By Myself, Yrs.
P.S. You are home, I think, but I continue
going

Dear,   February | Remind me again if you believe in God.

That was a rough patch, wouldn't you say? | I've made out signage of you. Silhouette
Feel better today moist fruitful information | profile apex of your trajectory. I look
at my fingertips. Are you looking for work | really hard among the bluff, clump &
still? Are you looking into my crossed | route.
hair, unnerving robbery?

The baptistery's oculus holed open to | _____
the elements (like the no envelopes). I met | _____
its eye for an hour. Bright hardly opening. | _____
Hannah & I bought tickets
for a sporting game. At the candle shop | You could be afflicted by dangerous
I bought 2 ornate. The cathedral pranced | diseases! & other dangerous despises.
as in Let's fatten every niche here.
The relic—we were the only visitors | Your virus, Yrs.
there—the Saint's disembodied head.
Sewn eyes, lip detach. At least it aligned
with ecstatic rage of the walls, mosaic,
fresco. & this: holy.

Dear,   February | by a sheet of bullet-proof glass to
                                         | prevent contact & ruin. When there was
Yesterday as I ventured to the sweet | no barrier, hostile hammers cheapened
shop, it started to rain dirt. It's the sand | the matter. Always create a cast years
wind, coming over the sea. I wonder if | before, & restoration will recreate.
you ever walked on any of that, packed
it for me & sprung tail. | We split up after the museum &
                                          | wandered among the proper
Nosy to witness relationships when I
get back. | _____
                                          | _____
                                          | _____
Obelisks here allude to the separation | & fashionable. Hilltop relaxing. At
of light from darkness, & the plaza's | the fountain, a demonstration regarding
appendages almost invade pity. | the climate, so we left promptly. I am
                                          | ignorant of what position
Sometimes the sculptures are encased | the participants advocated.
                                          | Residual energy, muscular exterior, Yrs.

Dear,   February   know? (Yrs.)

From the seat of the world.
The places of ill repute—a car's rear
lights. On arrival, visited the most
illustrious living quarters, secret shelved
along prescribed path. You could have fit
up there. The mission: avoid anti-climax,
recover luggage tags. The mission: learn
extracted depart. The mission: figure your
posture. The mission: sell back
the beneficial electronics & move on.

Will finish this tomorrow—unnaturally
exhausted suddenly. Must be all that
pondering The Mission.

There's a word for your idea, don't you

_____
_____
_____

Dear, February	suitably planned zone
ambush	
ambush	_____
	_____
	_____
ambush	
ambush	
	All Is Concealment. Surprised?, Yrs.
ambush	

Dear,   February | me. Have gone a different south now:

No memory confidence & so I note
as much as I can: eat, eat more, Yrs.; sleep,
Yrs.; mind muzzle velocity, Yrs.; don't
worry, Yrs.; you're okay, Yrs. Can you
mount a mare? I have, & you gotta dig
down the heels to stay on, dig 'em down
into the air. Then it's panic at nothing,
Dear.

On the road again, Dear. Decide on stakes.

The way you speak, smooth as a surgery,
to be spoken low, below tables, above
the mantle, between strips of möbius &

The kiosk sells long-distance packages.
Fed an addiction there, loitered, & had
subsequent self-restraint breakdown.
Thought about Joey & how it was too soon

_____

_____

_____

to think about Joey. He guessed extreme
weather—we both aspired to a career in
meteorology. We liked similar events, we
liked similar analyses & language. At
the City Hall, I found out about the reserve
& the Native Friendship Center.
Appropriately Ceremonious, Yrs.

Dear,   February

Excuse me, Hi, I stopped a woman walking
her dog to ask where the reservation was &
turns out I was ON it. Visited the Band
Office & wrote down facts in my notebook.
The reservation is self-sufficient. No
sidewalks because they don't use
them & the waiting list is long. These days
I collect earth samples, as I know you do.
Josh, the kid from yesterday, said you can
hear the glaciers shift. How far until it
goes? Made my way across the bridge &
found the festival celebrating a particular
vegetable. You would have loved it!
The traditional meal occurred at 5:00 p.m.

Do you suspect it is a tactic, the nomad's

anthology? Do you consider anyone's yard
semi-shielded or more? Modifications of
your stylized form mean Escape. Do you
vandalize or natural? Depends on intent.
Do you appreciate shared mammalian
features with me? Depends on program.

_____
_____
_____

Categorize according to digestion. You
swallow you chew you ruminate you there
trespass reservations & backyards.

Tomorrow I leave very early.

Etymologically Famished, Yrs.

Dear,   February

How long have we written? Now I'm
islanded—arrived as safe as one could
expect. I'm the city east. Bought bottles
of water & changed money already, tried
the coffee. Darker. I want to find things
here unavailable there, darker. Hiked lava
fields & asked how you would navigate
the terrain. Erosion, the biggest problem.
Went into a cave & experienced
physiological response. Traced
the perimeter of a gigantic crater, teetered
on edge. Names here must be approved
at birth. I know of a few places like this.
I ate wild wheat right from the ground &

hallucinated that I simultaneously stroked
your sleek head, going down. I had gifts
in mind, indulged the self instead. If you
look at the earth from above, shadows
turn profiled & throw you off. You sound
like a jerk requesting

_____
_____
_____

what's Typical. I dined at the restaurant
with friendly sophistication advertised.
This city is famous for its nightlife.
A dense white cloud sat on the mountain
as I left the nightclub. The sky was pink,
levelly, Yrs.

Dear,   February

Hey, Dear, do you find the historical
present practical? I took a Super Truck
with the guide to a mostly barren field, two
mid-sized rocks, noses touching. You
would have tapped the crevices. Then to
the isolated shack to change into full-body
suits, overshoes, special gloves; we rode
rocks out to the periphery, then embarked
on our separate vehicles. The gear keeps us
warm & we receive a brief lesson from
the guide. Vigorous day. The spring boils
audibly. A meet at the swimming pool, so
we don't get to go in.

The farmer, though, lets us into his green-
house to stand among the rows.
Compulsory naked shower before entrance
to the geological pools. You may be
caught then. It smells strongly of sulfur;
you may be overpowered, Dear.

_____
_____
_____

The insular is overpowering me, Dear.
Hightailing it again.

Ushered, Yrs.

Dear,   February

In a cloud all was white. Distance & size
undistinguishable. Sky ground follow
the dot which is the person leading
bigger slow down smaller speed up.
Reckless steer, you use your hands
to maneuver. My helmet round & blue
hard dot.

My company, your eyes are read,
describes the whites.

Relatively weak bonds to deform in. I
plan to eat & change soft toothbrush
every recommended 3 months; clean
the cleaner, it rinses with inevitability.

I attempt repeatedly to beat my personal
best & the group's while I'm at it.

Just don't know when to stop, injured
picked grin chew the lessons.

_____
_____
_____

Bloodlines, what have you done? Cheek-
&-cheek races.

I'm displacing & sweating I think I
really need to talk about my day &
nights where have I been, there's some
internal wreckage, hard blue dot the only
point, joke's on who, I was so close
to saying, but sth. tells me you've got
skyline.   Yrs.

Dear,   February

Dear. How are you? A speech tic here
is Sorry: sorry this, sorry that. Makes me
feel sorry & subterranean.

Would you like to move to a homestead,
coastal & fortified, with me?

I had to ask. We will lavishly sorry all our
copies. We will count hills where kings
crowned & manage multiple counties
together. If pre-stone people were such
magnificent engineers, what's to stop us
from building temples & estates
of glamour? We will create ideal living
conditions for ourselves. Just let me

know. One set of emotions will be replaced
by another when I get the news. We will
arrange precisely the entrance stone.

When I had the fight with an Important
One, there was a little less love for me.

_____
_____
_____

We both learned, sorry, to whittle beside an
unidentified knee. The people here made
a weak adhesive of ox blood & horse tail.
It worked well enough to hold together
a stone wall in the moat area. The tapestries
are exquisite.

Easily Accessible, Yrs.

45

Dear, February	What/who/where are you a testament to?
2 continents in one go this time. Bear with me—it gets puzzled. Flight delays all flights. Decadent apartment buildings, except the outskirts. Attended a live show at night, fireworks, 98-year-old theatre still functional. Black screens on bottom level behind which widows could sit & listen to the performances, as being seen & in mourning was cultural taboo. At the cemetery tour, my favorite was the unmarried adult woman who insisted on burial with her parents in a mausoleum & had the door cemented over. The itinerary did not include this stop. The cemetery is worth a visit as testament to the determination of human creation.	When was the last time you peered behind the bark, & did you find a resource there? _____ _____ _____ Let's talk soon, really talk. Markings are the evident way we communicate. Yours, Yrs.

Dear,   February | bags, hold your ticket & ID, they can't go
                                   | past a certain point with you, but others are
My preferred little bounder. | trying to do the same thing. Dear, it
                                   | can be so hard.
I was away for the last round. Can you
please tell me what it was like? My | After registration & meeting others,
memory mainly cradles
the cacophony & the shells after adults | _____
happen. Or were you not around? | _____
                                   | _____
I am thrilled you are part of my
information, you part of my list. | I had dinner & a headache. The plane had
                                   | 2 stories, flying house. Through the woods
The security lines make goodbyes | (looked for you even though I knew you
awkward. Did we ever say Goodbye? | couldn't be there), down some steps &
You have to keep moving, move your | into town. Dirtbikes clamor—mosquitoes.
                                   | Vaccines, signing documents. Yrs.

Dear,   February

Cold again, & my own bathroom. Official
village welcome; the red stockings girl had
#1 footwork. Even when people know you
don't speak their language, some will sit
you down, take both your hands & talk
a digging. The village school is on a hill
where the sheep graze. 2 dogs mated on
the sidewalk in front of my house. One had
bloodshot eye (the top dog). Both stared
baldly as I passed. Dani says I have no
problems with pronunciation.

Storks everywhere—I just made
the connection btwn. the whoop cries &
them. Woke to an urgent kingdom
in the street.

Language for a few hours after, after
phone frustration.

More language, & a hike to the reservoir.
Postcards scattered about dated 1972. (!)
Funeral procession stopped the village

_____

_____

_____

today. Tomorrow is a name day.

Wish we could celebrate together. Kate,
Pat & I perused the menu options
gleefully; the waitress informed us, after
a good 10 minutes, only one item was
available.   Range, range, range, Yrs.

Dear, February	don't foresee. Peppi's sister told me to sleep until lunch tomorrow, as it was

Dear,   February

Salutations, Dear. Falling into roles expected b/c they are expected. Please don't think because I have so much going on that I do not want to hear how you are. The President visited our village & spoke in the square, but I did not understand. They really love eternal flame here. Answered questions for a radio interview in the language. Pat's trainer told him she noticed I speak in paragraphs. At the old church there was a massacre & mothers tried to dig water for their children. One boy told me he loved me today.

The board resists chalk, a problem we

don't foresee. Peppi's sister told me to sleep until lunch tomorrow, as it was raining & gorgeous to do that. I guess others share this delight of mine—slightly disappointed, b/c sometimes you want to think you invented. R. died &

_____

_____

_____

a) learned it while watching news in the language/images, gradual affirmation,
b) things are happening there?,
c) I happened to be in the kitchen then.

Free To Visit, Yrs.

Dear,   February | have you seen it?

Peppi's sister (still don't know her | I'd rather miss the happy things.
name) & I walked the reservoir |
removed. After the potato field is | Dust collects rapidly here, trail of mass-
a small chapel. She went in & stood | acre.
before the offerings—flowers. I heard | _____
her speak, Thank You, I heard my | _____
name. I looked at the water. You can | _____
see another country from the mountain | Cooling-off streets downtown: spot-
peak. | lights left on vending stalls, entire lines
| of illuminated dirty water bottles, caps
Please do not give me news in list | off, intricate arrangement. ??? Finally, I
format, with bullets. Formality | knew: day's flower vendors.
depressions. Those are the miles. |
The Time of Parting is canonical— | Centrally, Yrs.

Dear,   February

The body: the part I skip to sometimes.
Whether here now. There?
I like the gendered language. It means
you've noticed at least one feature when it
feels like nothing. How you describe
depends, look.

From down here, the soaring appears easy.

The radio in my kitchen is impossible
to turn off; this morning I woke to opera
in the language.

There's a metal grate over the front door—
I think you could squeeze through, you
alone. The film projector I found in
the closet is not functional, nor the cassette
player. Wasn't it your Independence Day?

_____
_____
_____

My landlady brought salties. The girls
dress like they're much older, economy
nestled in so deep.

I could read the school sign. Before, I
could not. Adjustments visible against
the static.
Purchases, one by one, Yrs.

Dear, February	How can we react when you request orderly fixing?
I have noticed:	
Scaffolding—standing on a grave. The temporary is underrated, & you suspect relief is located there, while I with my pointer trace the oblong through a filmy window.	_____ _____ _____
The fire escape—something between us.	
Scaffolding—drapery to climb, to dangle. I form a fist around the most severe angle & argue it.	
	You Like It Barefoot, Intimate, Yrs.

Dear,   February

You intimated I owe you; you intimated
we both lacked what I owe you; I am
bewildered & halt, headlit—I disappoint
with debt but cannot seem to move.

_____
_____
_____

Yrs.

Dear,   February

Oh, you. Main predators & natural
predators don't necessarily overlap. So
many formalities with the documentation
process. They stamp officially. I ironed
my clothes with my new iron & killed
a roach, my hiking boot weapon.

Woke in the middle of the night to
a distinct chomp. Hunted it with eardrums
thrumming to find the source: invisible
life in my bed frame, feeding on the wood,
on my sleep.

They fear wanderers here. Witnessed one
being refused café service.

Visited Kate at the lake & her 70-year-old
neighbor unearthed pictures of his dead
wife. Of course, she was not dead
in the photographs. Boys at the bar sent us
drinks via the server, then barely

_____
_____
_____

acknowledged the act.

I observed the kids at the orphanage. Yard
so overgrown they kept losing their shoes.
Schedules, Meetings. Yrs.

Dear,   February

The public service industry here could use
improvement. Gets dicey when it comes
to counters.

There used to be electricity & water
regimens. You would not know about
that. My landlady reminded me of heat.

This morning I washed an apple &
wanted to eat it, but bit like dirt & earth,
so I opened the kitchen door to the terrace
& pitched it over. Then I proceeded with
the other 2. Perhaps you'll find them one
day piled in sticks below, gifts, although

gifts missing introduction do not have
quite the same impact.

The final days preceding a crucial date
have a way of simultaneously muting &
amplifying.

_____

_____

_____

Information is learned here by word
of mouth. That's how it rolls. Few of my
questions are answered, but I gather
flexibility & burrow passages.

Forage, Yrs.

Dear,   February

I count weekly here. Do you remember
puberty? So hormone-driven, all extra
energy & the ludicrous processes. Would
you believe the Twin Rules? If one takes
an entrance exam & passes, even if
the other one fails, both are admitted. They
each serve half-time in the military.

The kitchen will be the room to keep
heated. I attach New to things that
happened before I left, even though
the word is inaccurate. A New movie,
a New band.

My laundry froze the line last night.

Crash course in HOW TO DO THINGS,
like a door off hinges, with Eric. A girl
at the bar said I had Too much fingers
in my mouth. Major, uncanny intersection
of neuroses. I can hear again, which is
better (eardrops). There's a name day for

_____
_____
_____

those without a particular name day. I shift
how I hold the writing implement when I
write in the language. I am uncertain as to
how you would deal with the waterfall
terrain near the hydroelectric plant. One
shape in the rocks—sloth aspect.

Glove, Yrs.

Dear,   February

Hi, Dear. I thought the claw-toy game was
chicken on a spit, which illustrates my
trouble decoding at a glance. Mixing
brownie ingredients: I found a stone!
The munificent friend prompted, Is it
a sugar-stone?

People here wave from the train or bus
until theirs are out of sight. I'd rather make
clean cuts.

Vacation cancelled. The road to the border
country was closed (snow). Drifts taller
than I am. Being outside, the cold makes
my nose bleed.

People like to pet my earmuffs—I think
only kids wear them here (& me). Snow
inside my building. Stairwells. How
the bird stands when you spot the first
of the season determines your year's fate.

_____

_____

_____

Wear red tassels until then. On our night
out, Sylvia requested the anthem
& dedicated it to me. A check-out girl
at the grocery store broke the tacit rule
of no comments on customer purchases.

They do notice what almost brushes their
waist, Yrs.

Dear,   February

Maybe I need a template to learn how
to say the right things. Are you gracious
in your accepts & declines? I've been here
for what seems like a while now. I
returned dictation & Valentin lit that shit
on fire. Not flame as you know it, but
indoors, mastered on leash. Dear, I was
sick from the containment.

They plaster trees with death notices
at specific intervals. To learn of a death so
visual. Obits you seek; these—eye level
trees, windows, shop fronts, doors, posts,
same basic format. & you: find supple dim
corpse, unless it's whisked from the wood.

_____
_____
_____

Track the days & post replacements. They
disintegrate with exposure to elemental.

My regards to family, subfamily, etc.

Yrs., mulling

Dear, February	surface almost unbearable. This, because my tank broke.
Funny—your taxonomy, so like the affair I use in my workspace & in my person's body.	Are you keeping warm?
Your markings distinct & rich, make me want tactile. Do not alarm.	Population shrinkage here: costly to pro-
	_____
	_____
	_____
Glandular eyes, glandular eyes, Dear, thank you for the glandular below the eyes.	create, plus the steady leaving. Disappearance of the citizens. N., cutter, brilliant, sees silence; hopped
My landlady taught me how to use the electric coil: bucket of water, drop it in, plug it in, leave 5 minutes, unplug & remove. Temptation to touch deadly	a gate walking me back (night) & discerned me a bouquet from a stranger's garden.
	Plucked Music, Yrs.

Dear,   February

The clear bags, assault to my dignity. You
wouldn't know, but what everyone sees
can tell. I sneak my refuse to the bin &
hope for privacy. How is it to live natural
& without shame?

Took my project to a nearby village,
sketch to the metalworkers. They'll help.

Grapefruit, dark chocolate at 6:20 a.m.,
then met with the dance troupe for
another festival. Dear, they suited me in
traditional garments, my contribution
to honor ground, embroidered threads'
weight. Sweat in creases, mine/others'.

Tourists got my picture in the thaw;
I opted for the dance b/c not afraid.

In some cultures, it is good luck to be shat
on by a bird.

_____

_____

_____

Dear, it would mar
your immaculate coat.

Summers, children had tasks: collect
certain herbs (weighed), paper to recycle
(weighed). Lists in shops for acquisition.
People were happy b/c they did not know
what in the world. Sincerely Good Luck,
Yrs.

Dear,   February

The walls could talk. Not poor, just
overwhelmed. Mixed levels—everyone
knew at least something, though:
pervasiveness. Go down to reach
the cistern & via aqueducts the liquid.
Does a sister's rigidity also contain
the malleable. Do your siblings wash
glass. Mosque carpets get vacuumed.
The young boys wear dress-like garments
on circumcision day & celebrate. Do they
know what they're in for. The junkyard
dog, familiar with junk & yard. My
landlady helped me hang laundry
on the line last night when I returned
from my brief trip.

Says mothers teach daughters order: best
clothing row 1, underwear never in front.
When a man considers marriage, he
moseys by his object's balcony to assess
skill. At the microbiology lab (or was it
the ethnography lab), workers boil

_____
_____
_____

tests in pots. The walls could talk. Stray
dogs roam the alleyways & eyes look real
mean.

Does absence ring your underbelly.
Yrs.

Dear, February	Please come bearing practical gifts.
Requesting your presence.	Please do not come bearing arms, nor catalogue of synthetic accessory.
WHO: Yous	
WHAT: Hibernation of the Most Cherished Variety	_____ _____ _____
WHY: If Yous Have to Ask	Hope to see you then.
WHERE: Planet Sleep	
WHEN: Any Day Now, or Already	R.S.V.P. A.S.A.P., Yrs.

Dear,   February

Allow for my appreciative reciprocity
with the planar here. They, the planes, give
to me & I care for the cartouche of their
scuffs. We speak when we want without
prompts, & it is nice.

House rules say the living room always
explicates gentle mixed with a healthy
dose of the violent.

If you do not love articles assuming
their accurate dwellings, you will lose
your footing during darks.

We do not use spit & chafe to turn atlas
pages. We respect globular pressures,
cleanly explore honed grids' invite
correlations.

House rules say reading & porcelain
combine solely in my mouth, only

_____

_____

_____

contaminated sometimes. Here we separate
according to sound. Here we run our hands
over matter with rags every so often. Here
we anticipate comfort & immunity: we
tape down the clean, use agents to unclog.
We eliminate deposits formed over
the months, the head's soaked & changed,
you see.   Severely, Yrs.

Dear, February	Maybe you cut me to the quick.
Uninhabitable, persistent subtext shellacs fixtures. Uninhabitable to me is zero senses. Uninhabitable, let us get technical about tenant rights & repair's responsibility.	
	_____ _____ _____
Let's meet about no-fee mortgages or rents or however it is done, first agree pillows, bedding & values. I don't understand how it is done.	I recall & could diagram all the waves of my nights, successful consolidation.
Okay if you cannot decipher the attitude, neither can I: I just recite nuanced rules, work on my word problems, work on opacity's punctuation & queuing.	One of us circulates more satisfactorily & the other is aware. There are ways we form, deform habits, Yrs.

Dear,   February   The cold glasses my skin. I challenge
                                         penetration of your furtive hide.
Friendly fire divulges just who shoots.
Prettiness no good for injury prevention.   The news announced a Cold Holiday for
Position & identification vital signs.   the north. My landlady rang my doorbell,
Shall we tell. All of our garments could
almost be called armor. Mail, the inter-   _____
locking, mail, protect the zones im-   _____
possible to plate.   _____

                                         asked to borrow sugar—translatable
People here hold jobs inconsistent   trope, cook the holiday away.
with their training—there is not enough
work to follow the tricky hunt trail.   Instinctual body paint mixed from spices
                                          & water. We painted one another all dawn
                                          & huddled the radiator. No hot water, so
They tell me in the language how difficult slept the morning in vibrants.
the language is. They do not see
the humor in that. *I* should know. But   Yrs.
as pride burrows, cases collect.

Dear,   February   I am an acquaintance of a landscape
                                                painter, or a friend. He took me up
Driven rain café: a bird flies in the open   to his studio, all oil, said he thought
door, hits the window near us, flies   he had a nice eye & that he touched it
horizontal, connects with the opposite   every night before bed.
window & drops behind the couch. Our
server reaches with both hands
for the screeching bird, dismissal out   _____
the door. Transformation from toss   _____
to flight. Then she brings me my order.   _____

                                                The Perilous, Yrs.

Dear, March	
I have nearly figured out your operation.	
	_____
	_____
	_____
Please surrender my dislocated procession, which you hold, a rifle, & I will surrender sth., too. Or, have surrendered.	
	Impact of our season, full, tense.
	Now we can replace with some other order & ask: Too much for whose sake?
	Yrs.

MINed muzzle velocity

Acknowledgments

Many, many thank yous:

Elizabeth Spires, Madison Smartt Bell, Joanne Bleichner, Karen Hattrup, my brother Matt, Mr. Goldstein, Bulgaria, Joanna Underwood (for Fridays)

Mark Bibbins, Liam Rector, Jackson Taylor, Matthew Zapruder Jackie Clark, P.J. Gallo, Evan Glasson, Yotam Hadass, Jason Ueda

Nate Pritts, not only for your single-l-wonderful, singular love, but also for your very actual help

Matt Ryan, for your labor and responsiveness

Matt Mauch and Lowbrow folks everywhere

The editors of *Action, Yes, alice blue, Anti-, Blackbird, BlazeVOX, Bone Bouquet, Court Green, Dusie, Ekleksographia, Everyday Genius, GlitterPony, InDigest, interrupture, Robot Melon, The Scrambler,* and *Sink Review* have my gratitude: some of these poems first appeared those places.

About the Author

Leila Saad (2011)

Mined Muzzle Velocity is Jennifer H. Fortin's first book.

Her work has appeared in, among other places, *Action, Yes, alice blue, Blackbird, BlazeVOX, Coldfront, Copper Nickel, Court Green, Everyday Genius, GlitterPony, H_NGM_N, LIT, Sink Review,* and *TYPO.*

Dancing Girl Press published her chapbook *If Made Into a Law* in 2011. Another chapbook, *Nicole C. (Apartment 4)*, was published as part of the Dusie Kollektiv in 2011. Another is forthcoming from Poor Claudia.

With three other poets, she founded and edits *LEVELER.* She has been named a Finalist for the Poetry Foundation's Ruth Lilly Fellowship.

Fortin is a Returned Peace Corps Volunteer (Bulgaria 2004-2006). For more information, visit www.jenniferhfortin.com.

www.ingramcontent.com/pod-product-compliance
Lightning Source LLC
LaVergne TN
LVHW011409080426
835511LV00005B/455